enlightenment for
Lazy, Crazy Bastards

by Kiril Ravensong

Phoenix Publishing books may be ordered
through booksellers or by contacting:

Phoenix Publishing
51 MacDougal Street, #197
New York, NY 10012
www.phoenixpublishing.us

ISBN 0-9789443-5-6
ISBN 978-09789443-5-3
Printed in the United States of America

There are not words to express
The depth of inner quietude resounding
Through these canyons of thought -
This precious brevity.

- Tentetsu of Haiku

Kiril Ravensong

Warning: This book is all about sex and money. God and awakening will be discussed as well. This book has the potential to change your life and make you laugh. If you are offended easily or take yourself (or anything else for that matter) seriously, then put down this book, and go about your business as usual. Blessings to you.

Hello most honored reader, and welcome to the book,
"Enlightenment for Lazy, Crazy Bastards."

I am taking this moment to impress upon you, while you still have this book in your hands, why buying this book will save the planet, change your life for the better, and get you laid like crazy.

Yes, this book will get you laid. If nothing else, that's more than worth the price of a paperback and the few thousand trees it took just to advertise this nearly three and a half decade long sojourn distilled into profound-wisdom-made-easy-to-absorb by even the laziest, craziest bastard (or bitch) in this mad, mad modern haze of lost souls.

You see, you won't buy the book written by an established member of some self-help circle or book club selection of the month because that book will not get you hard core sex like this one will. How about easy money, you like that? Buy this book. This is the last book you will ever need if you are a lazy, crazy bastard (or bitch).

Easy money while lounging on your lazy ass, getting crazy laid by super sexy yoga goddess punk rocker chicks or whatever warped fantasy floats your new yacht. That's what this book is all about. Buy this book, steal it if you can't afford it, 'cause what you can't afford is to miss out on the secrets contained in these pages.

Sounds awesome, right? Of course it does. But it's total bullshit. That's right, I lied like crazy and now I'm coming clean. No more lies, just the straight up, down, and dirty truth. I'm a nobody. Spent a lot of time and energy being as much of a nobody humanly as possible. But I'm hungry and homeless and need income so now I have to be a somebody to live.

Problem is, I am a lazy, crazy bastard and I have spent the last twenty or so years hiding out as a spiritual-seeking-THE-truth-old-soul sort of person. In reality, I am a liar, a coward, a thief, a drifter, a loser, a fighter, a lover boy player, and a chaser of rich, sexy women who keep me like a sex toy poodle and I am between lovers at the moment.

There is no excuse for my behavior. My current poverty is entirely my fault and my fault alone. The lies above were shameless pandering to the driving insecurities that are typically used to manipulate people into buying things they neither need nor can afford. I personally wish that the authors of the books I read would be upfront about wanting more money.

So, in the spirit of radical honesty: I am literally homeless and penniless right now and I want you, honored reader, to finance my absurd lifestyle.

Why I am so useless continues to astound me. My agent thinks I'm brilliant. My former lovers think I am wonderful, terrible, crazy, lazy, wise, loving, and deeply sensitive. My parents think that I should either go back on my medication or beg the monastery to take me back into their Zen Buddhist fold. I just don't get why people think so damn much.

Thinking hurts my brain. Stress threatens to end my already weak will to live. Society's rules baffle me. Awakening is just way too painful for a being who is already so deeply sensitive to the e-motions of the world. All in all, I have done everything I can to live a life of service and pleasure and God. Mainly because it feels so good when I do, and so very bad when I don't.

Service rocks my world. I love seeing people laughing, playing, and celebrating life. Pleasure is what my musician's essence is designed for. When asked what instrument I play, my reply is, "women." As for God, well She and I have an understanding: I keep Her laughing and She handles all my travel arrangements.

So, now that we have an understanding about who I am, let me tell you what I really think about you, dear reader. I believe that you are bored out of your mind and yet you are capable of so many great and terrible things that it hurts my feelings profoundly that you aren't already getting the press coverage you deserve.

I believe that your play will get you paid and laid. I believe that your pleasure will open the doors of paradise on this repressed social order once and for all. I believe that you are angry as Hell that the world is so filled with war and poverty and there's just not enough fame and fortune in your life right now.

You are the power. You are the power that every government, every religion, every corporation is trying to seduce into playing their game, the one where you worship their thought-idols at the expense of your God-given destiny to raise the roof of starship Earth till the stars collide into new vistas of ecstatic revelations of Oneness.

I want you to recognize that you are the captain of your own destiny. If you are not getting the results you want in your life, then I am expert enough to tell you it's because you are a lazy, crazy bastard. There's no magic bullet book that will get you laid and make money from doing nothing. Some discipline is required.

But who says discipline is a hard thing? It takes discipline to be a lazy, crazy bastard (or bitch) in a society that's screaming at us to buy, buy, buy and work, work, work. It takes discipline to get so good at bringing women to ecstatic peaks of orgiastic pleasure so as to have one's choice of the hottest and wealthiest in the world.

This book is really about, above all else, being true to one's own self. We are all, in my highly unprofessional opinion, fucked up in one way or another. I have devoted 2/3 of my life to so-called spiritual pursuit when the truth is, I just want to write books, make movies, and paint pictures while getting paid and outrageously laid for these offerings.

This was going to be a brief introduction, but I got carried away again. My producer partner says this book is a brilliant offering. She wants me to write big blockbuster films for her to produce and for me to star in. This would be a lifelong dream-come-true.

Your purchase of this book is literally feeding a human life. The income from this work goes directly to the actualization of a young man's dreams. I want to personally thank you for taking the time to read this introduction, and for purchasing this book.

Love and Light,
Kiril Ravensong

Kiril Ravensong

TABLE OF CONTENTS

The discipline of being Lazy

my Ted is SO lazy

but no one even notices

people think that he's cute

and children listen to him

we could learn a lot from Ted

rock on, Ted

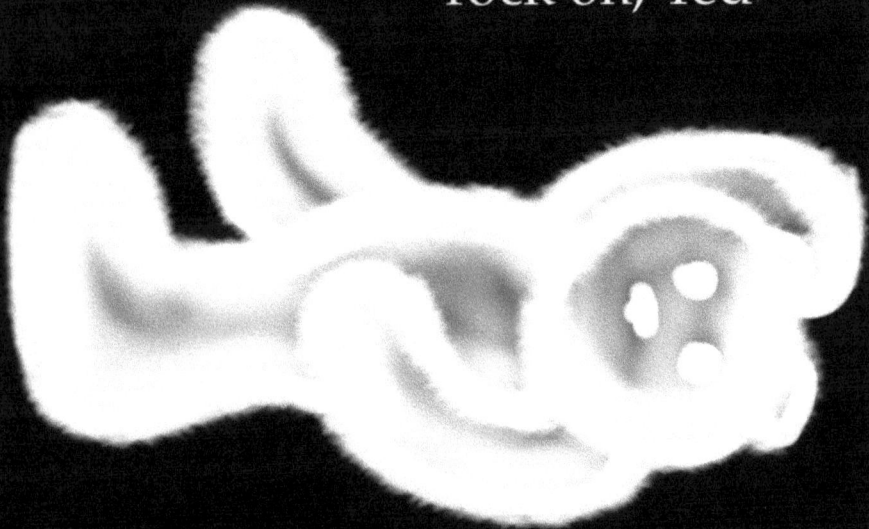

Instructions for fully enjoying this book:

Find a nice, cozy corner where you won't be disturbed. Have a cup of tea, or hot cocoa, and just relax. There's nothing to accomplish here, no great secret that you must be vigilant to grasp. Just a bit of lightheartedness in a world that, from my perspective, takes itself way too seriously.

Take a break from the seriousness. Unwind the stress of your life and read this book for the pure enjoyment of it. If you get inspired or have an insight, that's perfect. If you smile, laugh, or cry, that's perfect, too. Whatever comes up for you, just enjoy it.

It takes real discipline to be lazy. To simply let go of the "Go! Go! Go!" way of living can be terrifying for the Striver-Driver-Achiever. Yet, without deep relaxation, the body-mind literally gets worn out. Rest and total-let-go feels so good when we give ourselves permission to do only what feels good to us in any given moment.

Many of us do not know how to unwind our stress. Me, I'm a genius at it because I find stress so painful that I avoid it and unwind it as soon as it comes up. However, this type of unwind requires a profound willingness to be hopelessly lazy, at least once in a while.

To illustrate the point of Laziness to its most logical conclusion, the rest of this chapter is borrowed movie quotes and doodles. Enjoy.

(Ok, change in plan. My agent tells me that we need permission to use the whole host of really cool movie quotes I had planned for you. My future lawyer suggests I just go with the doodles. Rock on!)

Reality–Manifest!

Dream Seeds

Soul Symmetry

Nam Myoho Renge Kyo Nam Myoho Renge
Kyo Nam Myoho Renge Kyo Nam Myoho
Renge Kyo Nam Myoho Renge Kyo Nam M
Myoho Renge Kyo Nam Myoho Renge Kyo
am Myoho Renge Kyo Nam Myoho Renge G
Kyo Nam Myoho G

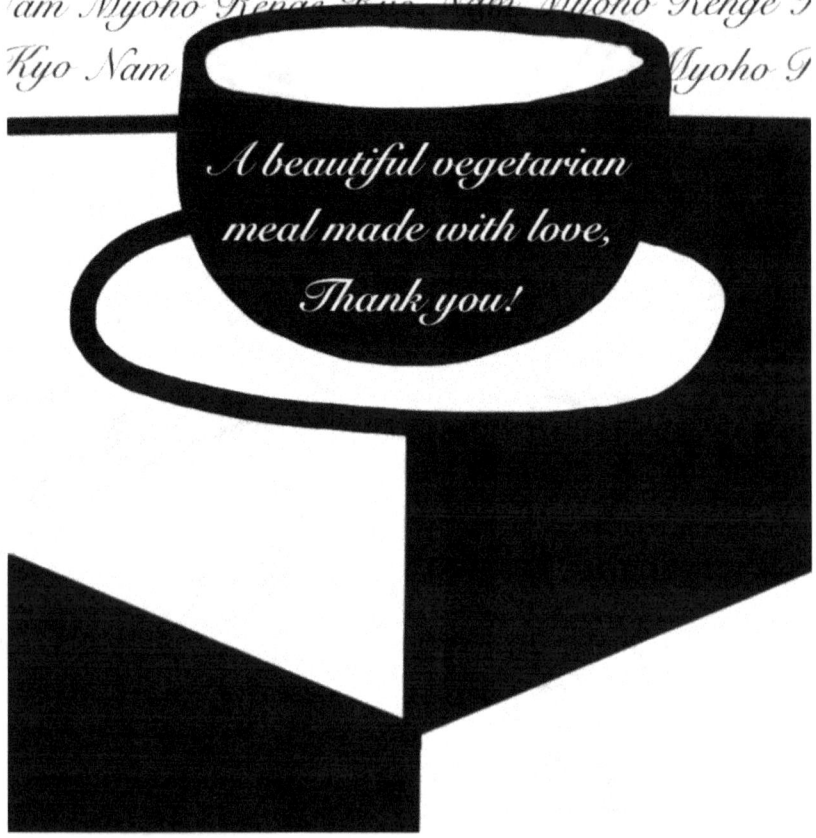

A beautiful vegetarian
meal made with love,
Thank you!

Journey

Mystery
Miracles
Magic

Any Dream you can dream,
No matter how things seem,
Really can come true,
So says Life to you.

The next page is left free,
For your dream
    to Be...
And so it is,
    Amen.

My Dream-come-true is...

how I long to live in the light of God...
  all that I am, all that I will ever be, Oh Lord God,
    hold me prayerfully in your fierce embrace,
      so that I might KNOW thee,
    and REMEMBER the Unborn Immortal within.
  I am yours, I am yours to be or to cease at once
  all thought-formations and return unto Thee
        WHOLE, HOLY and HEALED.

The genius of being Crazy

Kiss me! I'm Crazy!

You don't have to be crazy to be yourself, but it really helps. Mainly because there is a ton of social pressure to "fit in" and to not "rock the boat." The advantage of being regarded as crazy by one's peers is that it now gives you total, radical freedom to do and say whatever you feel like in any given moment.

It takes enormous amounts of energy to pretend to be something that you are not. Imagine what you could do with all that energy if it was devoted to your passions rather than figuring out how to not offend the terminally offended. Crazy means living a life of unreasonable glee, unhindered passion, and inexplicable laughter.

There's nothing wrong with being a lazy, crazy bastard. Nor is there anything wrong with the trying-to-fit-in and the strutting-around-like-a-real-important-somebody routine that most people seem so utterly absorbed with. There's nothing wrong with it at all, but it sure is an awful lot of work, and you are a lazy, crazy bastard after all.

Trying to be good, when all you want to do is coast through the semi-awake, daydreaming-Facebook-friend-me kind of life, is a very expensive lie to maintain. Examine how much of your actual time and energy is currently spent doing what you love, what you hate, and time-passing distractions.

As my Zeydah could have said (but never did): "Only a schmuck plants potatoes and prays for oranges."

So why not come clean and acknowledge that you are a totally incurable crazy person? It's cheaper than therapy, easier than dating models, and way more fun than living in perpetual fear of being found out for the lazy, crazy bastard you have already openly acknowledged that you are by buying this book. Oh yes, we know who you are.

The funny thing is, while you might have very valid concerns about being labeled crazy by your society, it is so unbelievably liberating to just drop the act once and for all. In that newfound liberation, you'll notice that no one is who they present themselves to be.

In a world where literally everyone is wearing masks, except for children, lunatics and masters, who seems happier?

Me, I am almost completely useless. There is not a single thing that I have ever done that did not end up in one preposterous failure or another. I was thrown out of the monastery and into a narrowly dodged 15-year prison sentence. I have been medicated for a decade for mental illness. My relationships are a disaster, my finances a joke, and my prospects are fairly dim.

The only difference between me and you, aside from the fact that you can afford this book while at the time of this writing I cannot, is that I am laughing at my self while you are likely busy defending your self with all you got. Why not relax, be your Self? Who knows, you might actually start to like the real you.

My ex-girlfriend hated it when I called her a self-indulgent, pleasure-seeking bitch. I don't know why, it was one of the things I enjoyed most about her. Perhaps it violated the image she was spending desperate amounts of energy pretending to be. It is astounding to me how much I myself hide behind crappy projections when, as far as I can tell, I am actually an incredible powerhouse of loving light in the world.

It's not about radical honesty either. I suck at that. Man, I can be such a chicken shit liar when it comes to being really vulnerable and straightforward with what I'm really thinking and feeling. Mostly, I just want to be liked. However, if people only like the fake me, then I can never relax. All that tension takes the juice out of living and I like getting laid way too much to live like that.

Better, in my mind anyway, to be reviled for my own garbage than revered for some phony act that I don't even understand. Don't get me wrong, I manipulate plenty and play ego games like an old Grandma trying to win at Sunday night Bingo. But what do you expect from someone who writes a book entitled, Enlightenment for Lazy, Crazy Bastards?

Since the whole world has no choice but to accept me exactly as I am, and will accept whatever it is that I consistently express, why not free myself from fear of judgment and dance through life like the village idiot? I can't be concerned with what others think of me, when I'm not concerned about what I think of myself.

Being crazy simply means that you don't fit into the roles that society currently has made available. Since society is merely a collection of random agreements between people pretending to be something they are not, I am really wondering why crazy is not regarded more as the compliment it is meant to be.

Lunatic means: one who desires to touch the moon.

And I say, "Why not?"

Not fitting in is great when the thing we can't fit into is a sinking ship of decaying values. No one felt bad about missing out on their chance to sail on the maiden voyage of the Titanic after its tragedy. But the same people were going crazy to get on when it was first advertised. I see society in the same way. A decrepit ship of fools on the ocean of universal consciousness.

Just one little unexpected bump, and the whole thing falls apart. Like a house of cards built by the side of the highway. Everything is going great, then one single car goes by, and down the whole thing comes. That's why the Awakened Ones tend to get lynched; their truth exposes all of our lies, and the whole game of our life comes tumbling, tumbling down in the presence of this truth.

Life is fun. Happiness is a virtue. Play is the best way to move money. Love is the answer, no matter what the question, love is the answer. Move towards health and happiness with style.

So who is the crazy one: The person who goes for their outrageous dreams and clings to those dreams like a life preserver in the social ocean of negativity, or the society that is over-medicated, undervalued, hyper-stressed, and openly unhappy?

If you want the truth, then you had better be prepared for the possibility that your whole life, as you now know it, will fall apart. If your identity is built upon lies, a lot can change with one simple shift to honesty. If every relationship you currently have is based upon you being someone you are not, any change you make can easily be misinterpreted as mental illness.

I spent a decade of my life medicated for mental illness before waking from the dream and coming back to my true self. I speak from direct personal experience. It is not to invalidate the field of psychology or psychopharmacology that I challenge the conventional notions of mental illness. My concern is better expressed by the experts themselves in the following proposal:

A proposal to classify happiness as a psychiatric disorder.

Source:
Department of Clinical Psychology, Liverpool University; June 18, 1992

Abstract:
It is proposed that happiness be classified as a psychiatric disorder and be included in future editions of the major diagnostic manuals under the new name: major affective disorder, pleasant type. In a review of the relevant literature it is shown that happiness is statistically abnormal, consists of a discrete cluster of symptoms, is associated with a range of cognitive abnormalities, and probably reflects the abnormal functioning of the central nervous system. One possible objection to this proposal remains--that happiness is not negatively valued. However, this objection is dismissed as scientifically irrelevant.

http://www.ncbi.nlm.nih.gov/pubmed/1619629

In the simplest possible terms, are you going to let the people who wrote this study determine the values by which you live your life?

To me, being considered crazy is a small price to pay for the total freedom to pursue "abnormal" happiness.

enlightenment
for
Lazy,
Crazy
Bastards

It's a Best-Seller!

Thank you so much, Honored Reader!

The freedom of being a Bastard

I'm a Bad Guy, Watch out!

As I write this text, my mentor, Martin Sage, is literally feeding me because I do not currently have the means to feed myself. And because I am a lazy, crazy bastard, I repay him for his kindness by stealing the idea for this book and really running with it. Now to be fair, the foodstuffs are items that he himself won't likely ever eat and all the ideas that Martin presents are stolen from somebody else anyway.

Actually, all of the ideas in this book are stolen from somewhere or someone. Some even come directly from my own warped experience. I will site the person when I flagrantly rip off their seemingly brilliant ideas, as best as I am able to recall, but not who they flagrantly ripped off their ideas from. That's their business. Actually, literally, that is THE business. I call it intellectual proprietary recycling.

I want to be upfront with you, on this issue anyway, right at the get go. Not because I am a person committed to radical honesty (I am), but because some seeming wisdom might, by chance, end up on these pages and impact your life in some meaningful-to-you epiphany. This scares the bejesus out of me, not because I am against your liberation (I am not), but because I am against being your liberator.

So let's get this out in the open, the great pink elephant in the Zendo. If you read this book, or any other, and have some kind of far out freedom experience or quit your job and join a commune with lots of sexy people or some monastery high in the Himalayas, then that's your business, not mine. My full-time job is feeding my skinny, white ass while chasing sexy, rich women.

When it comes to finding the right Guru, I can tell you only this: If the teacher knows that you are Buddha and they are Buddha and all is Buddha, then they also know that they are a crazy bastard talking to a lazy blockhead. Buddha does not go around seeking enlightenment or Zen or any other mental garbage like that. Buddha is Buddha. You are who ever YOU are. Get over it.

If this book is intended to accomplish anything other than entertain my laughing spirit or feed my starving body, it is to encourage you, most honored reader, to seize your inner lazy, crazy bastard (or bitch) and stop playing the blockhead game. The blockhead game is where everyone pretends to be everything that they obviously are not and no one gets paid or laid much at all.

I have lived the spiritual quest my whole life long. Trained on the mountain top with the Zen Master (awakening guaranteed, some post-monastery life assembly required), studied Shaolin Kung Fu (can still do the finger pushups to prove it), had sex with sultry, bendy Yoga instructors (God bless New York City), and otherwise dodged responsible job life with profound acumen.

So, as much as this makes me a spiritual expert in your eyes, I assure you, you have missed nothing. Everyone is an insane, full of shit, ego-arising killer ape with a direct connection to the ultimate benevolent power of the boundless eternal ocean of universal consciousness. If you wanted to wake up then you would have. Since you haven't, let's just focus on getting paid and laid, shall we?

Paid is good. It means eating, and playing, and having a nice place to live. Getting paid a lot for doing the little one already compulsively does is considered genius to our deluded culture, but really it's common sense. If you meet a spiritual type of person who is against money (if they have none, they're against it), then run! Do not stop to ask them the meaning of life, they don't know.

Getting paid to play with the raving fans I love the most is the business game I want to play. Having amazing sex with women that I am ecstatically attracted to, while adoring them with genuine worship and gratitude is the relationship life I enjoy most. Even the act of writing about this gets me into a great state! I notice that getting paid requires the same focused intensity, genuine service, massive drive, and responsiveness to feedback that getting laid requires.

With all these complaints I hear from employees, employers, and customers in the workplace, as well as from men and women in the bedroom, it seems that everyone feels that they are settling for less. How is that even mathematically possible? At least half the people out there have got to feel like they are getting more than they deserve.

While this book is all about getting paid and laid, it is not going to instruct you on sex. That's just stupid. Find someone you are attracted to and do what feels good until one or both of you starts calling out to God. Sex is the only activity that gets atheists crying out to their denied creator. God IS sex.

Getting laid is not important for your health or your well-being. It's essential for your life. No sex means no vitality, no juice, no real point to this whole embarrassing existence without it. Forget this Tantra crap or trying to make sex into something it isn't. Sex is sex. Life without sex is bitter and lonely. So take it from me, it's all about getting paid and laid until it's about something else.

That something else might be death, or awakening, or true love, or a tsunami, or even meeting a shark while windsurfing on some exotic shoreline. In those rare moments, your entire being will be mercifully absorbed on something other than your self pandering egoistic ways and you will be spontaneously capable of miraculous feats. Until then, however, it's all about getting paid and laid.

As for getting paid, here is the magic formula, courtesy of the infamous Internet Marketing Guru Frank Kern:

Person A provides person B a product or service.
Person B gives person A money.

For fun and easy living, you can even have person B give person A the money first. Then person A can eat while providing said product or service. Clever isn't it?

Just as this book will not instruct you in sex, this book is not going to instruct you on how to make money either. Mainly because if I really knew how to do that, then I would be doing it myself right now.

Even if this book makes me a millionaire, I am not sure that I would know anymore about making money than I do right now. The moment I figure out the art of moving money, I promise to write a book explaining it in great detail and will send it to all of you for free.

(My future lawyer will likely grind their teeth over that last statement, but seriously, if I truly master the chi of money, then the least I can do is to share the wealth of knowledge with my raving fans, right?)

Until that time, I will simply stick to writing about the things I love most to write about. If I wrote about what I actually know, then this would be my first and last book.

Man, what a lazy, crazy bastard I am. I wonder if any enlightened wisdom is getting through my block head and onto the page? If you have a really profound awakening experience, please put up a YouTube video about it.

Put in the title, "Yo, Kiril Ravensong, I'm _____ Enlightened!" Please use your newfound illumination to fill in the blank with something super clever, so it stands out, OK?

The most entertaining video gets something cool. Not sure what, and while I don't want my future lawyer to have ground down teeth, it will definitely be worthy of a Fellow Enlightened Lazy, Crazy Bastard.

In case the making money thing wasn't clear enough,
I drew a diagram. Enjoy it with my compliments.

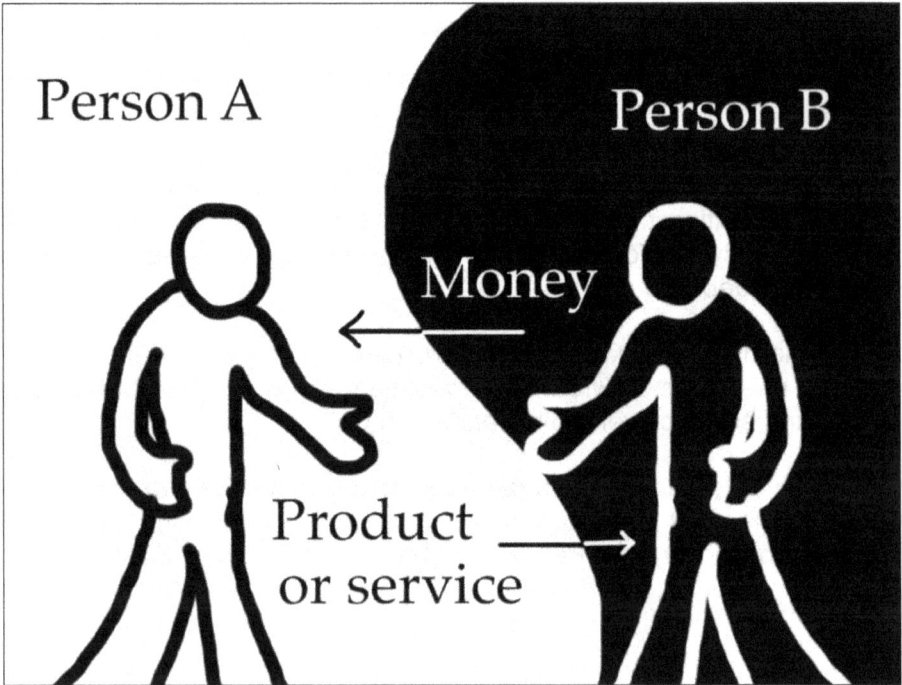

For directions on the sex thing, please consult the Internet,
which was invented for the distribution of free Porn.

Even Bastards need love

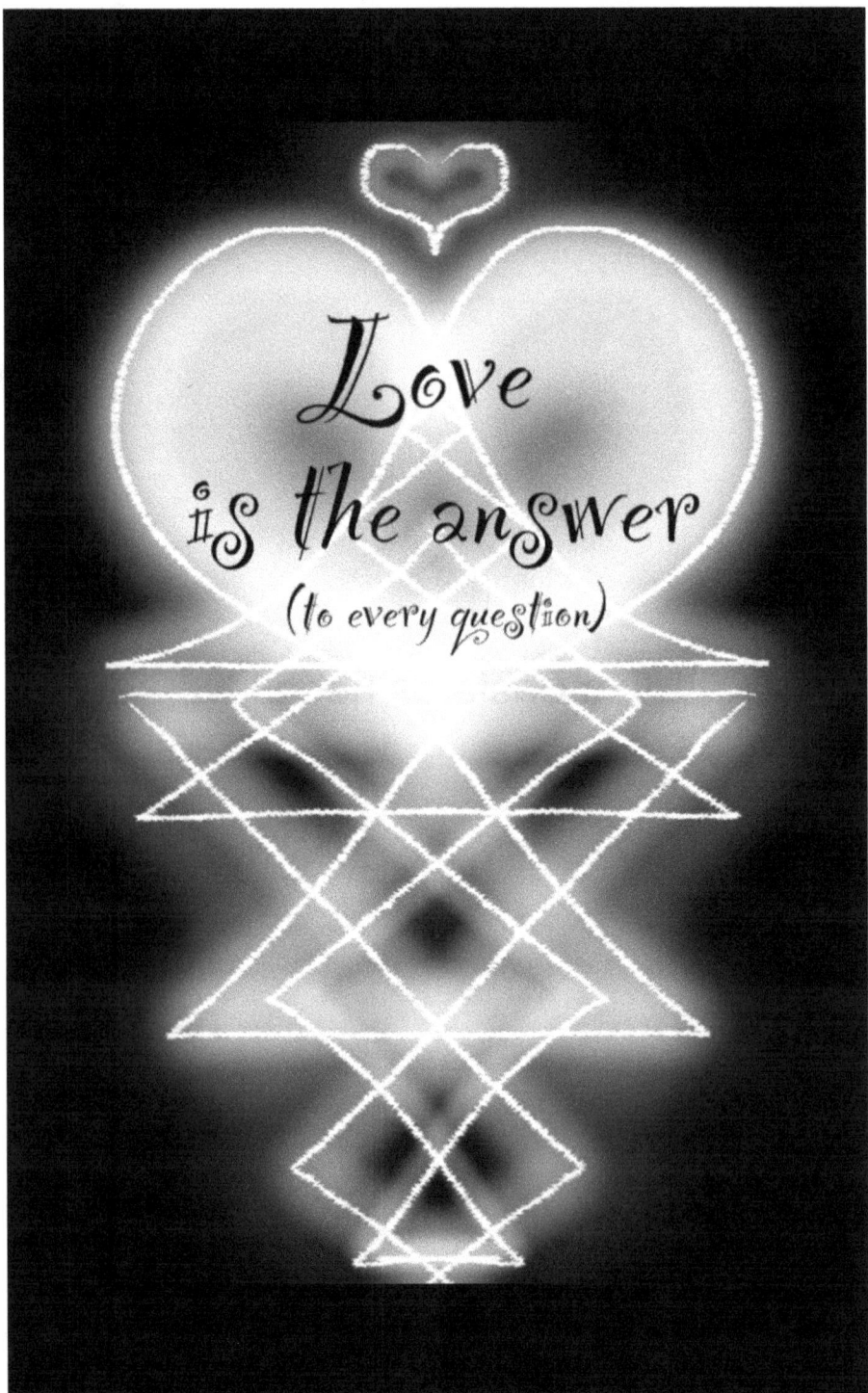

Love
is the answer
(to every question)

It may be rather forward of me to say this, as we likely have not even met as yet, but I love you. I love you more than I love myself. If I am totally honest, the combination of deep personal sensitivity and the overwhelming pain of humanity renders me mildly suicidal. Left to my own devices, I am an utterly useless, spastic, and dysfunctional catastrophe waiting to happen.

But I love. I love humanity. My love for humanity and my anger with humanity's stupid insistence on systems of unnecessary suffering have inspired every major and minor breakthrough in my life. The very act of writing to you is born of my genuine desire to spare you some of the pain I know that you are already in. How I love you, beloved reader.

More than the sustenance your patronage provides, it is your curiosity in these areas of life transformation, self discovery, natural being, and effortless liberation that provides the motivation to share all that I am. Everything, everything I am, I lay bare in these words in the desperate crazy longing that you will smile, or cry, or chuckle out loud and know my love.

It is so crazy alone to be awake. It is so crazy lonely to be asleep. After nearly three decades of struggling to awaken and stay in the awakened state, I am humbled by my utter failure to do so. The awakening experiences have come, washed away the old dreaming life, only to be gradually replaced with the next, albeit much happier, dreaming life.

Perhaps there is a magic Guru who knows the words to wake up the whole dreaming world from our self-imposed nightmare. I am not that person. I am the child pointing at the naked Emperor and the naked clergy, politicians, corporations, and all those other crazy cultists that make this world way too complicated for a simpleton like me to function in.

Mostly I get spanked for my efforts. People just don't want to give up the hallucination. I don't blame them one bit. Reality is bright and liquid and empty of conceptual handholds. The light hurts my eyes, the liquidity disorients my sense of self, and the lack of conceptual truth overwhelms my heart song with the rapture of angels singing. The truth-seeker act has failed me completely.

I have spent over two decades cultivating the spiritual arts. It may seem like I don't value these arts at times, but the truth is, I absolutely do. I love meditation, I love martial forms, I love yoga, I love writing and painting and ecstatic dance and moving chi! I have spent so much time and energy in these pursuits BECAUSE I love it so damn much.

The whole spiritual thing is a dead end, not because the techniques don't work, they absolutely do. The problem is that as long as we are avoiding being who we actually are, how will we ever benefit from even the most powerful teachings in existence? If I were to sum up my core understanding, accumulated over the bizarre course of my existential journey, it would be this:

Reality is Inherently Perfect

Reality is inherently perfect and we are perfectly OK in our myriad personal imperfections. When the imperfections are seen as occurring within a field of perfection, what's the problem with our not being perfect?

Reality is perfect because there is nothing other than Reality. Non-reality is a hallucination born of imperfect thinking arising in the present mind field of actual perfection. How rockingly irrefutable is that?

Everything else is just silence killing noise to me. In fact, the whole book is summed up by Reality's inherent perfection. That's it folks. Close up the book, use it for kindling or wiping your butt or whatever. No more crazy wisdom from this lazy bastard. You don't have to enlighten but you can't keep hoping that some stranger is going to tell you what you already know in every fiber of your being.

I love you, beloved reader. More than I love my own self. Me, I treat like garbage sometimes. You, I revere as the reason why I still insist on dragging this scrawny corpse through yet another day of this splendidly awful, awesomely tragical comedy of erroneous mistaken identity that we all agree to call life. Life is good. It really is.

Just follow your heart, and be good to yourself. I love you and no matter how good or bad things may get, I am cheering for you.

The next series of images illustrates the process of turning our problems into offerings. I drew them today just for you. Enjoy.

why me?
why me?
no more
no more
suffering
suffering
suffering
suffering
suffering
please
make
it
stop
suffering
suffering
suffering
suffering
suffering
help
help
help
suffering
enough
no

breakthrough

Self Ownership

ME

leadership

The yes and no thing

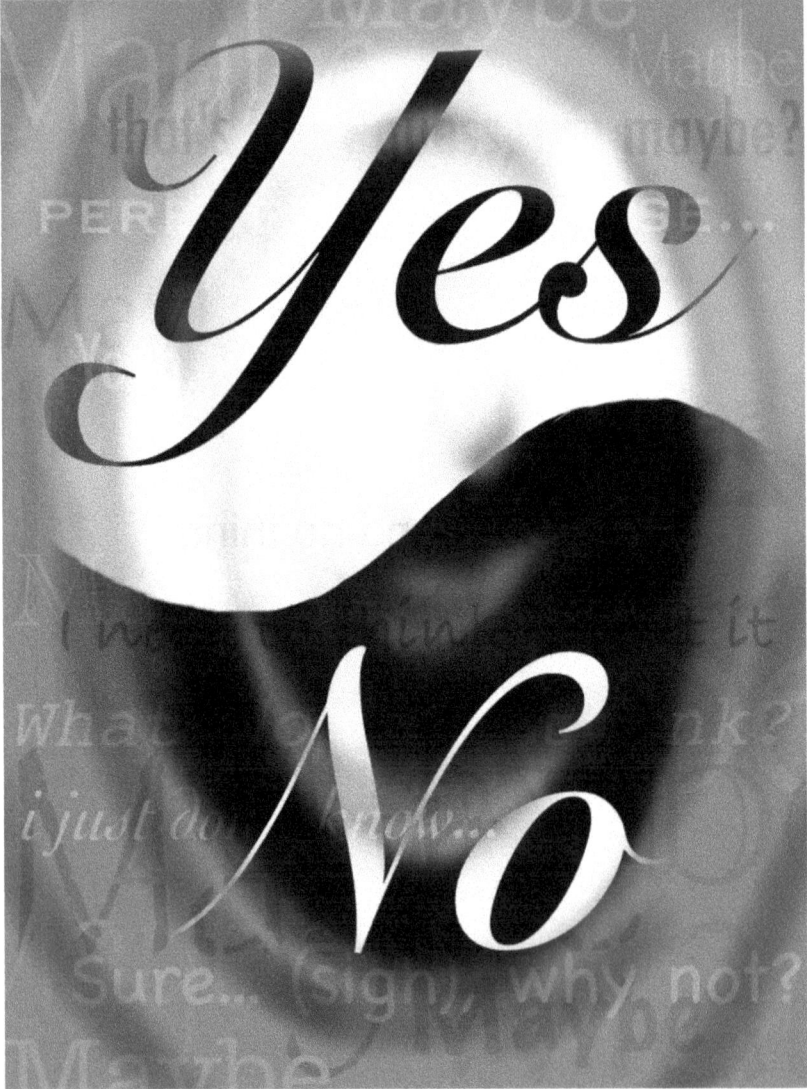

There are times when things simply do not feel all that good. Sometimes we seem to be at a total loss as to what the heck we are doing here on earth. In times like these, there really isn't much that can be said. All the same, since I'm in one of those times in my life right now, I just have to write. The pain and confusion all gets channeled into the words to the page. Let's see what comes next.

The challenge to being a lazy, crazy bastard is that one does not fit in very well with the usual sort of living that most of the people in our society seem to manage for themselves. On the plus side, the vast majority of those people are openly miserable in their lives, whereas the lazy, crazy bastards seem to live a comparatively stress free flow-with-the-wind-type-of-life.

There really does seem to be a better way to do things, doesn't there? If there is, then I personally have not yet found it. It's not as if I am intentionally rebelling against society or anything like that. I just find it more stressful to try and fit in than I do to be homeless at times while finding my own path through the world. The discomfort is temporary and natural.

It is the unnaturalness of modern social thinking that seems to generate so much stress. Doing things that do not feel good for long periods of time in order to earn a pitiful paycheck just does not sound like a trade worthy of a human being capable of great and terrible things.

Only by being true to one's own nature can the intensity of passions overflow into creative leaps and courageous bounds.

While I have heard many great-sounding theories and ideas on the subject of mapping out the internal human condition from various coaches, teachers, and gurus, my personal experience tells me that if it's too complicated for a three year old to remember then I will never use it when under direct duress. To that end, I have boiled it down to just three little words that we all know:

Yes = Vitality, aliveness, joyousness,
passion, pleasure, excitement,
growth, success, essence.

No = No way, no how, nope,
not gonna do it, no, no, no.
Thanks but no thanks, see ya later.

Maybe = Stress, inner conflict, indecision,
confusion, frustration, limbo,
crappiness and blah, blah, blech.

In my mind, when a crisis arises in our life, it's the *Maybe* getting so loud that it can't be ignored. **Yes** is easy, we all want more **Yes**. <u>**No**</u> is simplicity itself, <u>**No**</u> means <u>**No**</u>. <u>**No**</u> protects and clarifies our **Yes**. **Yes** to money, <u>**No**</u> to robbing banks. **Yes** to soup in soup bowl and poop in toilet bowl. <u>**No**</u> to poop in soup bowl and soup in toilet bowl. The *Maybe* is that whole shadowland of grey muck that distracts us from vital purpose.

Maybe is one part of our being saying **Yes**, and another part saying <u>**No**</u>. Which is actually a ridiculous waste of energy as well as a lethal source of stress. This *Maybe* does not exist anywhere else in nature, other than in modern humanity's psyche. This *Maybe*, in my opinion, is at once the barrier to our self liberation and the presence of liberation itself. *Maybe* is Hell and also simple feedback.

Remember how in grade school it was OK to skip school, or go on a trip, or even get out of gym class if you had a permission slip?

What if you had a permission slip for every aspect of your life? Would that assist you to feel better about saying **No** to spirit-slaying stress and **Yes** to your dreams-come-true?

I, Kiril Ravensong, give you permission to live the life of your dreams.

By the Author-ity invested in me by my creative license and the audacity inherent within my beating heart-song, I grant you the freedom to say *"**Yes!**"* and "<u>**No!**</u>" to anyone and anything you wish.

Life is too long to endure even one moment of unnecessary drama.

To whom it may concern,

This person has absolutely no excuse
for their inappropriate behavior what so ever.
As the author of the Best-selling book,
"Enlightenment for Lazy, Crazy Bastards"
I have officially given the holder of this form
permission to live their life in what ever
manner that best honors their true nature.

Thank you for your understanding.

Kiril Ravensong

PS: If you have any questions about this note,
please feel free to purchase my book. Thank you.

This person is going to die (someday) and is now absconding from all personal responsibilities for their remaining time upon this Earth.

NO.

No way.

Nope.

No, no, no.

N - O !

Never.

No.

NO.

NO.

NO!

NO!

No, thank you.

This person is certifiably insane. Please forgive periodic bouts of radical honesty, social impropriety, persistent irresponsibility, and inexplainable laughter.

This person has been diagnosed with an incurable desire to live the life of their dreams.

Please support their commitment to Passion, Service, Play, Laughter and Total Joyousness.

This person is allergic to stress and must be excused from all stress-inducing activities.

WHEN THE BODY SAYS, "YES!" THE SOUL SINGS

THEN, THE BODY CAN FOLLOW THE PATH OF LIGHT

GLITTERING ON THE WATERS OF CONSCIOUSNESS

It's all, and I do mean All, about Me

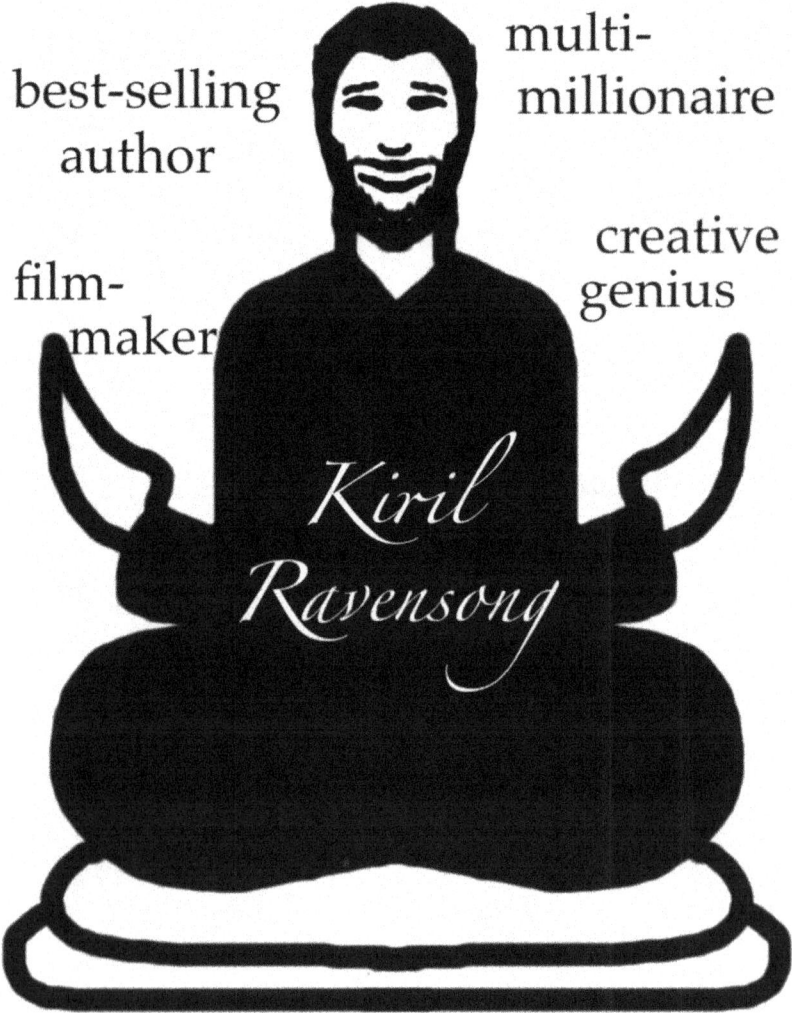

best-selling
author

multi-
millionaire

film-
maker

creative
genius

Kiril
Ravensong

You see, my fellow lazy, crazy bastard (or bitch), all of life is a stage, and we each are the stars of our own little universe play of consciousness. In simple terms that even a young child can grasp with great humor, "It's all, and I do mean All, about **Me**." You may have thought that it was all about something else, maybe even about you, and that's understandable, of course.

But the truth is, "It's all, and I do mean All, about **Me**." The sun rises and the moon sets for **Me**. Every human being on this spectacular Earth, including you, has been put in their respective roles for the sole purpose of serving my every whim and need. Arrogant, you say? Deluded, egotistical, selfish even? Perhaps, perhaps; but still, "It's all, and I do mean All, about Me."

World War I and II? Yep, "It's all about **Me**." The Great Depression, the death of Buddha, the birth of Jesus, and the Roaring Twenties! You guessed it! "It's all, and I do mean All, about **Me**." The creation of the cosmos, the end of all time and space, the New York Stock Exchange and those cool little tropical islands everyone wants to visit? "It's all, All, ALL, about...**Me**."

Now that we have this all cleared up and squared away, one might naturally wonder what's the point of that little tirade or who the hell is this lazy, crazy bastard, but that's not really the right question. The real question in my mind for you is, "How does this help **me**?"

A former business associate of mine and I had the following argument:

Businessman: You always make everything about you.

Me: Why would I ever do that when it's so clearly all about **Me**?

Businessman: There you go again! All about you!

Me: No, all about **Me**.

Businessman: That's what I said!

Me: I thought you said, "all about you?"

Businessman: You never make it about me! Never!

Me: I always do. Always!

Businessman: Never!

Me: Always!

Businessman: How can you say that, when you just said--

Me: It's all, and I do mean all, about **Me**!

Businessman and Me: [in unison] Exactly!

I'm not sure that guy ever got the joke. Some people take themselves so seriously. Here's the quick cure for kicking the taking-one's-self-too- seriously habit:

For men: Take a very cold shower then look at yourself naked in a full length mirror. If that doesn't do the trick, show your girlfriend, wife, or the maid.

For women: Imagine your boyfriend, husband, or ex doing the exercise above. Then remember how seriously you still take the things that guy once said to you.

For gay, lesbian, transgendered: You fabulous beings already know this, but an easy reminder is to look at all those "breeders" arguing, cheating, and divorcing while "protecting" the institution of marriage.

Once you no longer take yourself so seriously, you are free to dance upon the stage of life! Free to take your place as the star, the focal point of all existence, the shining, shimmering center of the unfolding movie of your life journey.

"It's all, and I do mean All about **Me**."

Say it out loud a few times just like this: "It's all, and I do mean All, about **Me**." Say it to yourself while looking in the mirror as it takes a bit of daily practice and some intelligent selfishness to fully own it. But once you own this marvelous little gift, and can state out loud with total sincere authority, beyond any and all doubt, no matter who else is in the room, be it your lover, the President of The Un-tied States of America, or your mother, looking each person square in the eyes with a smile on your lips, that "It's all, and I do mean All, about **Me**..."

Oh my, the games we will play!

Then you will stop worrying about that job, that boring sex partner, that state of the union address, or what ever stress-inducing activity you momentarily feel that the world has unreasonably placed upon your shoulders and just relax. Fuck 'em if they can't take a joke and fire them if they can't get with the simple program: "It's all, and I do mean All, about **Me, Me, Me**."

Now go on out there and play in the world of delight you find yourself in today. You are lazy, so stop this looking busy nonsense and go have some fun. You are crazy, so quit trying to impress phony people with phoniness that impresses no one. You are a bastard (or bitch), so don't bother pretending to be nice, you're not and now you know that "It's all, and I do mean All, about **Me**."

Wealth and Zen for the Lazy, Crazy Bastard

DANCE —

Into the zendo
Twilight maples
Come [dancing]

- Soen Nakagawa

Let's talk frankly, shall we? This next section may end up chock full of utter nonsense that sounds really good with the occasional dirty pearl of wisdom stolen from wiser men and women than myself. This is channeled straight from my warped head onto the page, mainly because I need this information. I honestly have no idea what I am going to write next. So, diving right into Wealth and Zen...

The problem with both topics is that I clearly know nothing about either one. Right now, I have such a profound poverty staring me in the face that I am baffled by my utter lack of concern. Penniless in a foreign nation with no clear time frame for income to come in nor an outcome that doesn't involve me sleeping outside.

I could seriously benefit from some Zen and Wealth right about now. So, what can I say about either one without waxing poetic or sounding desperate to fill my head with false hopes instead of my belly with food and my wallet with cash? Real Zen Wealth, then, would be the exact opposite of whatever I am doing right now.

Right now, I am fasting and coming to center. There is nothing artificial in what I am doing. This is my genuine best effort to care for my own body-mind. I am writing like crazy and actually loving every minute of it. This may well be my favorite project that I have ever worked on. This is fun and it's such an easy activity.

How funny, even though I have no idea what I will do to sustain my life, I am feeling more urgent that these words reach you. Both because the activity is so damn enjoyable and because it is the best thing that I can think to offer with the resources I have available to me right now. Perhaps this is Zen Wealth after all.

Perhaps, everything is fine, really fine right now, and this is the natural flow of life for a lazy, crazy bastard such as myself. Perhaps, this is the inevitable course a life runs: we do everything except the one thing that God put us on Her great green Earth to do until we reach the place where nothing short of a miracle will save us.

And we are that miracle. We are the miracle that we waste so much time looking for outside of ourselves.

You are a miracle to me. If you bought this book, you are literally feeding my body, my heart, and my very essence. If you are reading these words and finding the courage to live your own dreams or face your inner demons, then you have made all my suffering meaningful. I can gladly endure my current predicament knowing that it makes your life a little bit better.

There is so much love in my heart, I am dying with the inability to express myself with the totality of my love. My love for you, for your pain and your gifts, your flaws and your brilliant luminosity. I am dying to this moment because my heart is cracking open and these words are spilling out with my tears. So much grace now.

I have been suffering alone in silence waiting for some clear sign that I am enough, enlightened enough, articulate enough, smart enough, good enough, to present myself to you, most beloved reader. Please forgive me for waiting so long to raise this voice. I have been listening to the sorrow and laughter for so long, of you and our fellow humanity.

I know not the ways of Wealth. I am a poor man rich in spirit. I don't know anything about Zen. I eat when food and hunger occur at the same time. I sleep wherever the most comfortable place becomes available to greet my weary body. Everything feels so clear right now. What a radical change in state, all phenomena are merely the stuff of dreams.

How funny it is to finally see this now. These thoughts dance upon the veil of mind, the same veil of mind upon which the gathered perceptions of reality are painted. The less thought-activity clouds the veil, the more clearly the Reality can be painted. But it is still not Reality, merely the absence of thought-activity. Reality is beyond concept.

What a lovely day it has been. What a miraculous life we share, honored reader. Be blessed, be blissed, and keep on keeping on.

So ring the bell that still can ring;

Forget your perfect offering;

There's a crack in   everything;

That's how   the Light gets in

- Leonard Cohen

Hey, the joke's on you, do you get it?

my Ted,
Colonel Red

Alright, so when I was a little kid, I assumed that everyone over the age of 6 was a complete idiot. To my unsophisticated child mind, adults seemed to be obsessed with defending their little stress tales at the cost of giving me the attention I knew I deserved.

After all, wasn't I the child prince of God Herself come to the Earth to inspire the sleepfull masses to awaken to the reality of Paradise never lost? Wasn't I the genius artist lover bard who once fell in love with the moon, a flower, and a butterfly all in one day?

I was a peanut wonder of playful antics and well-crafted inquiries into the lighter side of human existence. Amazing to see how much of our childhood efforts to get attention form the basis of our livelihoods and love strategies as adults.

Our deep self is very much like a child with vastly more power than our conscious minds can even believe. I believe that we can harness the power of this deep self by relating to our child selves with open-hearted curiosity.

When I asked my child self about what am I supposed to write next, this is what came to the page:

The Little Kid who Dared to Dream
by Kiril's inner child

These boring people are mad at me (Again!)
Because I don't follow the rules and I
Don't believe them when they tell me
That my dreams are "impossible" (Again!)

They call me a lunatic, a crazy person, a nut.
All because I draw pictures all day and dream
About real magic, and write silly stories, too.
That's OK, I don't mind it one bit, not me...

That's because I know that a nut is something
Roasty toasty and very good to eat.
And a crazy person is someone who can imagine
Way weirder things than anyone else.

But a lunatic, I didn't even know what
That word really means... So I looked it up,
And this is exactly what I found out:
That boring people wrote all the dictionaries.

Now I'll pretend that lunatic really means:
A magical person who can touch the moon.
So now, I just need to find the right spot,
To reach up and be a lunatic for real...

If I could touch the moon, then really,
There would be no more "impossible" at all.
I don't care about what people think, because
Dreams are more important than rules to me.

That's what I decided to do, all those years ago.
I spent my days mastering mystical arts and
Honing my imagination in the blue fires of faith.
Until I reached the day when "impossible" was gone.

Gone from my thoughts, gone from my heart.
All that remained in my mind, was exactly what I
Wanted most to do, to see, and to feel. Then,
I was finally ready to realize my childhood dream...

It was a magical adventure, more amazing than
Any of those boring people would ever believe.
That's because they read dictionaries and believe
In the words "impossible" and "crazy" and "nut."

But they don't know what Lunatic means,
Not one bit. But I do know, because I am one.
And just to prove it to you, that I really did
Touch the moon, I drew a picture of it here.

See, told you so. Now, it's your turn.
If you can think it and draw it,
Then you can do it for real; It's true.
Even if boring people say it's "impossible"...

Lunatic

Are you laughing yet? Do you get it? What is business anyway? Selling bottled tap water while sitting next to the fountain of youth. Same with spirituality, higher education, dating, and self help programs. The ideas are pointers at best. The customers are just as much lazy, crazy bastards as the ones peddling such nonsense. Lighten up, everything is going to be OK, and you are going die someday.

sometimes, I look upon this world and KNOW

that I am capable of doing so many

GREAT and TERRIBLE things...

to live this life, (☆)ne with the WAY,

is to give energy to that which promotes life.

for LIFE promotes that which in and of itself is

(☆)ne with the WAY, the way of LIFE.

One for the road...

Last chapter for this book. The temptation is to say something Important and Useful. To sound Wise and Impart Words of Wisdom to you, most honored reader. However, it's the last chapter! I simply love you too much to keep these pearls of personal insight and words of my mentors from you. Saving the best for last really rocks!

Facing our fears is neither easy nor hard. No one will think less of you for being your true self. Everyone will recognize when you are acting as less than you really are and will treat you accordingly. True vulnerability is required to achieve the state of intimacy from which all success naturally flows. Sex without intimacy is masturbation. Money without intimacy is poverty.

It takes real guts to be vulnerable, to speak our mind, and to be in touch with the e-motions we feel. It takes a great leap of faith to leave the familiar roads we know and travel the unique path of our dreams. The path winds through unknown territory and there are times when we must walk alone. I believe that life is inherently bountiful and genuinely fun. I believe in you.

I love being in service to you. This book is a pure pleasure to write. There are many ways that I could earn income. But it isn't about the money because that's not what actually motivates me. What gets my juices flowing electric is money earned through true intimacy with all of my rocking, raving, loving fans.

That to me is wealth beyond measure. It's fulfillment, love, radical financial freedom, living the dream life, the highest victory possible all at once!

We fear intimacy because it is scary to be that vulnerable. That's the reason why most people do not experience the love they long for, the love that they actually deserve to experience. Making money is not easy. If it was easy, then everyone would be rich. That doesn't mean that it is hard or that there is not enough for everyone.

All of God's creations have a place in Her divine plan. Every plant and animal has an integral place in the ecosystem. The main thing I take from my years of spiritual development is that all of life is unified through the infinite web of relationships. As Tony Robbins says, Life promotes that which is life promoting.

When I figure out the way to riches, I promise to write you all about it.

There is God, so get over it. She loves all Her creation and is the field of benevolence from which all phenomena manifest. We humans are made in the image of God, who is both masculine and feminine, creator and destroyer, one and not one. All the existence of God implies is that there is a living intelligence to existence as made evident by babies, orgasms, sunsets, chocolate, and every other yummy expression of love.

Religion is neither the problem nor the solution
to relating to the Reality of God and humanity.

Government is neither the problem nor the solution
to all humanity living together in harmony.

Consumerism is neither the problem nor the solution
to finding more fulfilling ways to live our life.

Spirituality is neither the problem nor the solution
to resolving the paradox of worldly duality.

As far as I can discern, the root of every problem and key to every solution is You! Only you can even decide what it is that you want and do not want. Only you can say *Yes* or **No** to the feedback of your efforts to find happiness, health, wealth, love, light, and laughter in your own life journey. Getting help from your friends and mentors only makes sense when you are clear in what it is that you actually want.

Death is coming for you. No need to be scared, She comes for everything and everyone. I only point this out because people seem to be waiting for permission to go for their dreams with every ounce of intensity within them. When we are confronted with a life and death matter, we do not wait around for approval.

I, Kiril Ravensong, officially give you permission to start doing something that makes your heart go pitter patter again.

Put butterflies in your stomach to know that you are on the right track. Enjoy the comfy places in life, but, as my NLP mentor Steve Linder says, "Comfort is like crack. It's addictive and it will kill you." If you don't know how to get butterflies in your stomach, then go up to the most attractive person you can find and tell them exactly what you would do to make them orgasm.

Alternatively, get on a stage and perform, especially if you have convinced yourself that you are not a performer or that you have no talent. Everyone wearing a human body bio suit is a performer pretending to be other than divine perfection. No one has talent, there is no such thing. All there is to talent is the willingness to make a loving impact on other people's life journeys.

Walk up to strangers and get to know their story. Strangers are friends that you haven't met yet. Friends are great, but allies united in a common vision or a rocking business game will make your life a flow of miracles. Get together with positive people you trust and admire to share your passion vision dream with. Reverend Michael Beckwith refers to these gatherings as Tell-A-Vision parties.

Everyone gets a turn to say some crazy dream they have, the more impossible and outrageous it is, the better. The point is not to be concerned with the how, rather to begin to reclaim our own Yes with our friends. Who knows what business games or compelling shared visions may emerge? You will simply have to try it out for yourself and see what happens. Isn't life grand?

Try to fall down or make a big mistake at least once a day. Really, really big falls or disasters count for a whole week. But when the week is up, resume making mistakes and pushing yourself to the falling down point. Success is failing until you succeed. Duh! That's how you learned how to walk, tie your shoelaces, or any other activity that you now do effortlessly. Have fun with your learning again.

Tony Robbins does this routine where he pretends to be the parents of a child who tried to walk but fell down instead. "Oh well, guess the kid is just not a walker. It's time to just give up on the little tyke." It is a hilarious way of conveying how absurd it is to not go after your dreams with the same playful, natural, joyous sense of exploration and growth that every infant expresses in the very act of learning to walk, talk and make it to the potty.

If life came with instructions, then we would all be rich, successful superstars living the life of our dreams. However, as Tony Robbins says, "Success leaves clues." Meaning that while there may not be instructions to life, there are laws to succeeding in every area of one's life. You need only find someone who is successful in an area you wish to grow in and study exactly what they do to create consistent successful results.

Actions speak louder than words but achieving actual results is what gets us paid and laid. Delivering actual value to our clients is what turns them into raving, loyal, loving fans. Delivering actual value to raving fans is what turns our work into getting paid to play. Martin Sage is a genius at helping people to design their ideal business game. This book is a prime example.

Every mentor named in this book has directly touched my life for the better. Each and every one of them is mentioned with the highest respect. They are people committed to excellence, integrity, service, and living their dreams. They walk their talk and that's very rare these days. I highly recommend checking them out. Coaching is a powerful tool to support stepping into your dream life. Definitely look into getting the right life coach if you haven't already.

That's it. For this little project anyway. All written while homeless and penniless on the beach of Puerto de San Miguel on the island of Ibiza, Spain while studying in the Sage University course, "Live Your Dream." Please feel free to contact me with questions, testimonials, love letters, and praise, whereas all complaints, criticisms, and hate mail get sent to my agent who finds such letters highly amusing.

E-mail: info@enlightenmentforlazycrazybastards.com

I wish you all the best in your life journey.
Be well and take good care of yourself.
Be blessed, be blissed; with Love and Light,
Kiril Ravensong

finis!

Whew...

I wonder what's next?

Hmm...

www.ingramcontent.com/pod-product-compliance
Lightning Source LLC
Chambersburg PA
CBHW072004060426
42446CB00042B/1829